Cracking the Code: To Credit Repair
And the Path to Financial Independence

Benjamin Blackwell

Copyright © 2023 by Benjamin Blackwell

All rights reserved.

No portion of this book may be reproduced in any form without written permission from the publisher or author, except as permitted by U.S. copyright law.

Contents

Introduction	1
Step 1: Believe in Your Ability to Fix Your Credit	2
Step 2: Gather Your Credit Reports	4
Step 3: Identify Derogatory Items	6
Step 4: Understand the Section 609 Credit Repair Secret	9
Step 5: The Power of Dispute Letters	12
Step 6: Follow the Step-by-Step Instructions	26
Step 7: Responding to CRA's with the 4-Step Letter Writing System	29
Step 8: Negotiating with Debt Collectors and Creditors	35
Step 9: Dealing with a Subpoena and Facing Legal Action	41
I. 100 Tips to Building Credit	45
II. Understanding Credit Score Calculation	54
Conclusion	58
One Last Thing	60

Introduction

Welcome to "Cracking the Code: To Credit Repair and the Path to Financial Independence," a book designed specifically for those who have spent years struggling with poor credit. If you're tired of feeling trapped by your financial situation, this book is your ticket to understanding that your credit can be cleaned up without the need for expensive attorneys or credit repair companies. In these pages, you will discover the incredibly easy process that professionals use to remove all derogatory items from your credit reports. No matter if you're dealing with charge-offs, repos, bankruptcies, judgments, short-sales, loan modifications, late payments, or collection accounts, this step-by-step guide will empower you to take control of your credit and improve your FICO scores from below 500's to above 700's. Get ready to learn what to do, when to do it, and how to do it, all in plain English!

Step 1: Believe in Your Ability to Fix Your Credit

Believe in yourself! You have the power to fix your credit and achieve a better financial future. It may seem daunting, but remember that many others have successfully repaired their credit, and so can you. Trust in your ability to take control and make positive changes.

Understanding that you have the capability to improve your credit is the first step towards success. It's time to let go of any doubts or negative thoughts you may have about your credit situation. Instead, embrace a positive mindset and believe that you can turn things around.

Take a moment to visualize the life you want to lead—a life free from the constraints of poor credit. Picture yourself being approved for loans and credit cards with favorable terms. Envision the relief and sense of accomplishment that comes with financial stability and freedom.

Remember, this journey may not be easy, but with determination and the right knowledge, you can overcome any obstacles. Have faith in yourself and your ability to navigate the credit repair process. By believing in yourself from the very beginning, you're setting the foundation for a successful credit repair journey.

So, take a deep breath and repeat to yourself, "I have the power to fix my credit. I believe in myself and my ability to achieve financial freedom." Embrace this positive mindset as you embark on your credit repair journey. It will serve as a guiding light, motivating you to stay focused and take the necessary steps to clean up your credit.

Believe in yourself, because you are capable of achieving incredible things. The power to fix your credit is within your grasp. Let's move forward with confidence and determination, knowing that a better financial future awaits you.

Step 2: Gather Your Credit Reports

Now that you've embraced the belief in your ability to fix your credit, it's time to gather your credit reports. These reports will be the foundation of your credit repair journey. They contain crucial information about your credit history, including any derogatory items that may be affecting your credit score.

To obtain your credit reports, you have the right to request a free copy from each of the three major credit reporting agencies: Equifax, Experian, and TransUnion. Thankfully, this process is relatively straightforward.

First, visit the official website of each credit reporting agency. Look for the section that allows you to request your credit report. It may be labeled as "Free Credit Report" or something similar. Click on the appropriate link to initiate the request.

Next, you will need to provide some personal information to confirm your identity. This may include your name, address, date of birth, and Social Security number. The credit reporting agency needs this information to ensure that they are providing the report to the right person.

Once you've provided the necessary information, you can choose how you would like to receive your credit report. Typically, you have the option to view it online or have it mailed to you. Select the option that is most convenient for you.

Repeat this process for each credit reporting agency to obtain a copy of your credit report from each one. Remember, you are entitled to one free report from each agency per year, so take advantage of this opportunity.

When you receive your credit reports, carefully review them for accuracy. Look for any derogatory items such as late payments, collections, or bankruptcies. Take note of each item that needs attention, as you will be addressing them in the upcoming steps.

Remember, your credit reports are crucial tools in your credit repair journey. They provide you with a clear picture of your current credit situation, allowing you to identify areas that need improvement. By gathering these reports, you are taking an important step towards understanding the specific challenges you'll be addressing and ultimately achieving a better credit score.

So, gather your credit reports and get ready to delve into the next steps of the credit repair process. Armed with this information, you'll be better equipped to tackle the derogatory items and pave the way for a brighter financial future.

Step 3: Identify Derogatory Items

Now that you have your credit reports in hand, it's time to identify the derogatory items that are impacting your credit score. These items are negative marks on your credit history, such as late payments, collections, charge-offs, or bankruptcies. By identifying them, you'll have a clear understanding of what needs to be addressed during your credit repair journey.

Carefully review each section of your credit reports from Equifax, Experian, and TransUnion. Look for any accounts or entries that show negative information. These can include:

1. Late Payments: Note any instances where you made payments after the due date. Late payments can significantly impact your credit score and should be addressed.

2. Collections: Identify any accounts that have been sent to collection agencies due to non-payment. Collections can severely damage your credit and should be prioritized for resolution.

3. Charge-offs: Take note of accounts that have been charged off by the original creditor. A charge-off occurs when a creditor writes off a debt as uncollectible. It remains on your credit report and continues to affect your score.

4. Bankruptcies: If you've filed for bankruptcy, it will be listed on your credit report. Bankruptcies have a substantial negative impact on your credit and require specific steps to address them.

5. Judgments: Look for any judgments against you resulting from a legal dispute or unpaid debt. These can negatively affect your creditworthiness and should be tackled accordingly.

6. Short-sales or Foreclosures: If you've experienced a short-sale or foreclosure on a property, it will be reflected in your credit reports. These events have significant implications for your credit, so it's essential to address them.

7. Loan Modifications: If you've undergone a loan modification, check if it is accurately reflected on your credit report. Ensuring that the modification is properly recorded can positively impact your credit score.

8. Other Negative Items: Pay attention to any other derogatory items, such as tax liens, repossessions, or public records, that may be listed on your credit reports.

By identifying these derogatory items, you'll gain a comprehensive understanding of the negative factors affecting your creditworthiness. Take the time to make a list of these items, including the creditor's name, the amount owed, and any associated details.

Remember, knowledge is power. Identifying the specific derogatory items enables you to focus your efforts on addressing and resolving them. Each item on your list represents an opportunity for improvement and will be addressed in the subsequent steps of your credit repair journey.

So, go ahead and identify the derogatory items on your credit reports. Make a comprehensive list, and get ready to take the necessary actions to remove or improve these negative marks. By doing so, you'll be one step closer to achieving a healthier credit profile and securing a better financial future.

Step 4: Understand the Section 609 Credit Repair Secret

Now, let's delve into cracking the Code of Section 609. This is a powerful tool that can significantly improve your credit score. Understanding this will give you the knowledge and confidence to challenge inaccurate or unverifiable information on your credit reports.

The Section 609 refers to a specific section of the Fair Credit Reporting Act (FCRA), a federal law designed to protect consumers' rights and regulate credit reporting agencies. This section grants you certain rights as a consumer when it comes to the information listed on your credit reports.

Under Section 609, you have the right to dispute any inaccurate or unverifiable information directly with the credit reporting agencies (CRA's). This includes any negative items that are dragging down your credit score. By exercising this right, you can challenge the validity and accuracy of these items, ultimately leading to their removal from your credit reports.

It's important to note that Section 609 is a legal and proven method for improving your credit. You don't need to resort to costly attorneys or credit repair companies to achieve results. Instead, you can take matters into your own hands and navigate the process independently.

By understanding and utilizing the power of Section 609, you become an empowered consumer. You gain the ability to hold the credit reporting agencies accountable for the information they report. This levels the playing field, giving you a fighting chance to clean up your credit and achieve financial freedom.

In the upcoming steps, we will guide you through the process of using the Section 609 effectively. You'll learn how to craft dispute letters and communicate with the CRA's to challenge the derogatory items on your credit reports. This step-by-step approach will equip you with the knowledge and tools necessary to achieve successful credit repair results.

Remember, Section 609 is your ally in this journey. Embrace it, understand it, and use it to your advantage. By doing so, you'll be taking a significant step towards improving your credit and reclaiming control over your financial future.

So, take the time to familiarize yourself with Section 609. Understand its importance and the rights it grants you as a consumer. Armed with this knowledge, you'll be ready to move forward confidently and start the process of challenging the derogatory items on your credit reports.

Step 5: The Power of Dispute Letters

One of the most effective tools at your disposal for challenging derogatory items on your credit reports is the dispute letter. Dispute letters serve as your voice when communicating with the credit reporting agencies (CRA's). They allow you to assert your rights under Section 609 and request the removal of inaccurate or unverifiable information.

Dispute letters are a written correspondence that outlines the specific issues you have with the items on your credit reports. They provide a clear and concise explanation of why you believe the information is inaccurate or should be removed. Crafting a well-written dispute letter is crucial for a successful credit repair process.

We have included four dispute letter templates that you can use as a starting point. These templates have been proven to be effective and will save you time and effort in crafting your own letters. Each template is tailored to address different types of derogatory items, allowing you to customize them to fit your specific situation.

When writing your dispute letters, keep the following points in mind:

1. Be Clear and Concise: State the purpose of your letter clearly and succinctly. Explain the reason for your dispute and provide any supporting evidence or documentation.

2. Include Relevant Information: Provide details about the specific item you are disputing, such as the account number, creditor's name, and the reason why you believe it is inaccurate or unverifiable.

3. Be Assertive and Professional: Maintain a professional tone throughout the letter. Clearly express your rights under the Section 609 and assert your expectation for a thorough investigation by the CRA's.

4. Keep Copies and Records: Make sure to keep copies of all your dispute letters and any supporting documentation you include. This will help you track your progress and provide evidence if needed in the future.

Now, let's provide you with the dispute letter templates you may need for your credit repair process. Please find the templates below:

Template for Challenging Late Payments:

[Your Name]

[Your Address]

[City, State, ZIP Code]

[Date]

[Credit Reporting Agency Name]

[Address]

[City, State, ZIP Code]

Subject: Dispute of Late Payment Reporting on [Account Name/Number]

Dear Sir/Madam,

I am writing to dispute the late payment reporting on my credit report regarding the [Account Name/Number]. According to my records and the terms of the original agreement, I believe there has been an error in the reporting of late payments.

Specifically, I contest the accuracy of the reported late payment on [date/month/year]. After reviewing my personal records, I have found no evidence of a late payment occurring on this account during that time. I have consistently made timely payments as agreed upon in the original terms of the account.

I kindly request a thorough investigation into this matter in accordance with my rights under the Fair Credit Reporting Act, Section 609. I expect the credit reporting agency to take appropriate action to verify the accuracy of this late payment entry.

Enclosed with this letter, please find copies of relevant documentation supporting my claim, including bank statements, payment receipts, or any other supporting evidence that proves my timely payment history.

I urge you to promptly investigate this matter and remove the inaccurate late payment from my credit report. It is crucial to ensure that my creditworthiness is accurately reflected in all future credit evaluations.

Additionally, as per my rights under the Fair Credit Reporting Act, I request that you provide me with a written response confirming the results of your investigation. This response should include any actions taken and the updated status of the account on my credit report.

Please consider this dispute letter as a formal request and a reminder of your responsibility to maintain accurate and fair reporting of consumer credit information.

Thank you for your immediate attention to this matter. I expect a prompt resolution within the statutory timeframe of 30 days. Your cooperation in rectifying this error will be greatly appreciated.

Sincerely,

[Your Name]

[Your Contact Number]

[Your Email Address]

Enclosures: [List the enclosed supporting documents]

Template for Disputing Collections:

[Your Name]

[Your Address]

[City, State, ZIP Code]

[Date]

[Credit Reporting Agency Name]

[Address]

[City, State, ZIP Code]

Subject: Dispute of Collection Account Reporting on [Account Name/Number]

Dear Sir/Madam,

I am writing to dispute the collection account reporting on my credit report regarding the [Account Name/Number]. I believe there are inaccuracies in the reporting of this collection, and I request a thorough investigation to address this matter.

Upon reviewing my credit reports, I noticed the presence of a collection account from [Collection Agency Name] with an outstanding balance of [Amount]. However, I am unaware of any debt owed to this collection agency, and I dispute the validity of this account.

I kindly request that you provide me with all pertinent information regarding this alleged debt, including the original creditor's name, account number, and documentation proving that this debt is valid and legally collectible.

Furthermore, I assert my rights under the Fair Credit Reporting Act, Section 609, which grants me the right to accurate and verifiable information on my credit report. I expect the credit reporting agency to conduct a comprehensive investigation into the validity and accuracy of this collection account.

In accordance with the law, I request that you contact the collection agency and verify the following:

1. The collection agency has the legal authority to collect this debt.

2. The collection agency has provided all necessary documentation to prove the validity of this debt.

3. The collection agency has followed all legal procedures required for collecting debts, including providing me with a validation notice within the appropriate time frame.

If, upon investigation, you find that the collection account cannot be verified or that it contains inaccuracies, I demand its immediate removal from my credit report. Failure to do so will be considered a violation of the Fair Credit Reporting Act.

Please provide me with a written response detailing the outcome of your investigation, as well as any actions taken regarding this collection account. Additionally, I request that you update my credit report accordingly to reflect the accurate and verified information.

Thank you for your prompt attention to this matter. I expect a timely resolution within the statutory timeframe of 30 days. Your cooperation and compliance with the Fair Credit Reporting Act are appreciated.

Sincerely,

[Your Name]

[Your Contact Number]

[Your Email Address]

Enclosures: [List any enclosed supporting documents, if applicable]

Template for Addressing Charge-Offs:

[Your Name]

[Your Address]

[City, State, ZIP Code]

[Date]

[Credit Reporting Agency Name]

[Address]

[City, State, ZIP Code]

Subject: Dispute of Charge-Off Reporting on [Account Name/Number]

Dear Sir/Madam,

I am writing to dispute the charge-off reporting on my credit report regarding the [Account Name/Number]. I contest the accuracy and validity of the reported charge-off and request a thorough investigation into this matter.

Upon reviewing my credit reports, I noticed that the [Original Creditor Name] has reported a charge-off on my account. However, I believe there may be inaccuracies in the reporting of this charge-off.

To ensure a fair and accurate representation of my credit history, I request that you provide me with the following information:

1. Verification of the original debt owed to [Original Creditor Name].

2. Documentation proving that the debt was charged off according to the appropriate accounting practices and within the required timeframe.

3. Verification that the reported charge-off accurately reflects the actual amount owed.

I assert my rights under the Fair Credit Reporting Act, Section 609, which grants me the right to accurate and verifiable information on my credit report. I expect the credit reporting agency to conduct a comprehensive investigation into the validity and accuracy of this charge-off.

If, upon investigation, you find that the charge-off cannot be verified or that it contains inaccuracies, I demand its immediate removal from my credit report. It is imperative that the credit reporting agency ensures the accuracy of the information it reports to maintain the integrity of my credit history.

Please provide me with a written response detailing the outcome of your investigation, as well as any actions taken regarding this charge-off. Additionally, I request that you update my credit report accordingly to reflect the accurate and verified information.

Thank you for your attention to this matter. I anticipate a prompt resolution within the statutory timeframe of 30 days. Your compliance with the Fair Credit Reporting Act is expected and appreciated.

Sincerely,

[Your Name]

[Your Contact Number]

[Your Email Address]

Enclosures: [List any enclosed supporting documents, if applicable]

Template for Resolving Inaccurate Information:

[Your Name]

[Your Address]

[City, State, ZIP Code]

[Date]

[Credit Reporting Agency Name]

[Address]

[City, State, ZIP Code]

Subject: Dispute of Inaccurate Information Reporting on [Account Name/Number]

Dear Sir/Madam,

I am writing to dispute the inaccurate information reporting on my credit report regarding the [Account Name/Number]. After reviewing my credit reports, I have identified discrepancies and inaccuracies that require your immediate attention.

Specifically, I have noticed the following errors on my credit report:

1. [Describe the inaccurate information in detail, including account names, numbers, and the nature of the inaccuracies.]

I firmly believe that these entries are incorrect and do not reflect my true credit history. I kindly request a thorough investigation into these discrepancies to rectify the inaccuracies promptly.

As per my rights under the Fair Credit Reporting Act, Section 609, I assert that it is the responsibility of the credit reporting agency to ensure the accuracy and integrity of the information they report. I expect your agency to undertake a comprehensive review and investigation of the disputed information.

Enclosed with this letter, please find copies of supporting documentation that clearly demonstrates the inaccuracies in the reported information. [Include any relevant documents, such as account statements, payment receipts, or correspondence.]

I request that you conduct a meticulous examination of the provided evidence and take the necessary steps to correct these errors on my credit report. Please remove the inaccurate information and update my credit report accordingly to reflect the true and verified details of my credit history.

Additionally, I kindly ask that you provide me with a written response detailing the results of your investigation, including any actions taken to correct the inaccuracies. It is crucial that I receive confirmation of the updates made to my credit report to ensure its accuracy moving forward.

Thank you for your prompt attention to this matter. I anticipate a timely resolution within the statutory timeframe of 30 days. Your cooperation and adherence to the Fair Credit Reporting Act are greatly appreciated.

Sincerely,

[Your Name]

[Your Contact Number]

[Your Email Address]

Enclosures: [List any enclosed supporting documents, such as account statements, payment receipts, or correspondence.]

Feel free to personalize these templates according to your specific circumstances. Remember, these dispute letters are powerful tools for advocating for the accuracy of your credit reports. Use them wisely and assertively to bring about positive changes in your credit profile.

With these dispute letter templates in your arsenal, you're well-equipped to challenge the derogatory items on your credit reports. Let's move forward to the next steps and learn how to fill out these letters effectively and take action to improve your credit.

Step 6: Follow the Step-by-Step Instructions

Now that you have gathered your credit reports, identified derogatory items, and understood the power of dispute letters, it's time to dive into the step-by-step instructions that will guide you through the credit repair process. By following these instructions, you will be able to effectively challenge and remove derogatory items from your credit reports.

1. Fill Out Your Dispute Letters:

Using the dispute letter templates provided earlier in this book, carefully fill out each letter according to the specific derogatory item you are disputing. Make sure to include all relevant details, such as account numbers, creditor names, and reasons for the dispute. Be clear, concise, and assertive in expressing your concerns and rights under the Section 609.

2. Gather Supporting Documentation:

To strengthen your disputes, gather any supporting documentation that validates your claims. This may include payment receipts, account statements, letters of correspondence, or any evidence that proves the inaccuracy or unverifiability of the reported information. Make copies of these documents to include with your dispute letters.

3. Mail Your Dispute Letters:

Once you have completed and reviewed your dispute letters, it's time to mail them to the credit reporting agencies (CRA's). Send each letter via certified mail with a return receipt requested. This will provide proof of delivery and ensure that your letters reach the intended recipients. Keep copies of the letters, as well as the mailing receipts, for your records.

4. Monitor Your Progress:

After sending your dispute letters, it's important to monitor your progress and keep track of any responses or changes in your credit reports. The CRA's have 30 days to investigate and respond to your disputes. If you receive any correspondence from them, read it carefully and take appropriate action based on their response. Keep all communication and documentation related to your credit repair journey organized and easily accessible.

Remember, patience is key throughout this process. Credit repair takes time, and it's essential to stay persistent and proactive. Follow up with the CRA's if you don't receive a timely response, and be prepared to provide additional documentation or clarification if requested.

By diligently following these step-by-step instructions, you will be well on your way to improving your credit profile and achieving financial freedom. The power is in your hands to take control of your credit and pave the way for a better financial future.

In the next steps, we will delve into how to respond to the CRA's, provide you with a four-step letter writing system, and share additional strategies to further enhance your credit repair efforts. Stay committed and motivated as we continue this journey toward credit success!

Step 7: Responding to CRA's with the 4-Step Letter Writing System

After mailing your dispute letters, it's important to be prepared for responses from the credit reporting agencies (CRA's). This step will guide you through the process of responding to their correspondence using the effective 4-Step Letter Writing System. By following these steps, you will maintain clear communication and maximize your chances of achieving positive results.

1. Read and Understand the CRA's Response:

When you receive a response from the CRA's, carefully read and analyze the content. Pay close attention to any information or documentation they provide regarding their investigation into your dispute. Understand their findings and how they have addressed your concerns.

2. Assess the Accuracy of the Response:

Compare the CRA's response with your original dispute and the supporting documentation you provided. Verify whether they have taken appropriate action to correct the inaccuracies you identified. Look for any discrepancies or inconsistencies in their response that need further attention.

3. Craft a Clear and Assertive Letter:

If the CRA's have not adequately addressed your concerns or if you believe their response is inaccurate or incomplete, it's time to write a response letter. Use the 4-Step Letter Writing System to craft a clear and assertive message. Follow the template provided below as a guide.

4. Send Your Response Letter:

Once you have completed your response letter, make copies for your records. Send the original letter via certified mail with a return receipt requested, just as you did with your initial dispute letters. Keep the mailing receipt and tracking number for future reference.

The 4-Step Letter Writing System:

Step 1: State the Issue:

Clearly and concisely state the issue or discrepancy you want the CRA's to address. Be specific and provide any relevant details, such as account numbers, dates, or erroneous information.

Step 2: Present Supporting Evidence:

Include copies of any supporting documentation that reinforces your claim. This can include account statements, payment receipts, correspondence, or any other evidence that validates your position.

Step 3: Assert Your Rights:

Assert your rights under the Fair Credit Reporting Act, Section 609, and other applicable consumer protection laws. Clearly state that you expect the CRA's to conduct a thorough investigation and correct any inaccuracies on your credit report.

Step 4: Request Resolution:

Politely and firmly request that the CRA's take immediate action to address the issue. Specify the resolution you seek, whether it is the removal of inaccurate information, the correction of errors, or any other necessary action to ensure the accuracy of your credit report.

Response Letter Template:

[Your Name]

[Your Address]

[City, State, ZIP Code]

[Date]

[Credit Reporting Agency Name]

[Address]

[City, State, ZIP Code]

Subject: Response to [CRA's Correspondence Reference Number]

Dear Sir/Madam,

I am writing in response to the correspondence received from your agency regarding my recent dispute on [date of original dispute]. After carefully reviewing your response, I have identified concerns that require further attention.

First, I appreciate your efforts in investigating my dispute; however, I believe there are unresolved issues that have not been adequately addressed. The discrepancy I initially reported regarding [describe the specific issue] has not been appropriately rectified based on the information provided in your response.

To ensure a fair and accurate representation of my credit history, I have enclosed copies of the supporting documentation I previously provided, along with any additional evidence that reinforces my claim. These documents clearly demonstrate the inaccuracies in the reporting and further substantiate my position.

I want to remind you of my rights under the Fair Credit Reporting Act, Section 609, which grants me the right to accurate and verifiable information on my credit report. It is imperative that you conduct a comprehensive re-evaluation of my dispute, considering the evidence I have submitted.

In light of the discrepancies identified, I kindly request that you take immediate action to rectify the inaccuracies on my credit report. I expect a thorough reinvestigation of the disputed items and the necessary corrections made accordingly. It is crucial that my credit report accurately reflects my creditworthiness and financial history.

I trust that you will handle this matter promptly and in accordance with the law. I kindly request a written response within 30 days of receiving this letter, detailing the actions taken to address my concerns.

Thank you for your attention to this matter.

Sincerely,

[Your Name]

Remember to customize the template with your specific details and tailor the letter to address your unique situation. Stay persistent and proactive throughout the process, maintaining organized records of all communication and documentation.

Step 8: Negotiating with Debt Collectors and Creditors

When facing a proven debt, it's essential to address the situation proactively. Negotiating with debt collectors and creditors can help you find a manageable resolution and potentially reduce the amount you owe. This chapter will guide you through the step-by-step process of negotiating in plain English, providing tips and techniques to help you achieve a favorable outcome.

Step 1: Understand Your Financial Situation

Before initiating negotiations, assess your financial capabilities and determine the maximum amount you can afford to pay. Take into account your income, expenses, and any other financial obligations. This understanding will help you establish realistic negotiation goals.

Step 2: Communicate with the Debt Collector or Creditor

Reach out to the debt collector or creditor to open the lines of communication. Here's a template for initiating contact:

Dear [Debt Collector/Creditor],

I am writing to discuss the debt owed to [Creditor Name] and explore possible options for resolution. I acknowledge the debt and am committed to finding a mutually agreeable solution. I am currently experiencing financial difficulties, and I am interested in discussing a potential settlement or payment arrangement that fits within my means.

I would appreciate your willingness to work with me to find a fair resolution. Please let me know how we can proceed to address this matter.

Sincerely,

[Your Name]

Step 3: Negotiation Strategies

a. Offer a Lump Sum Settlement: If you can afford to pay a portion of the debt upfront, propose a lump sum settlement. Start by offering a percentage of the total debt as a one-time payment, emphasizing that it's the maximum amount you can afford.

b. Request a Payment Plan: If paying a lump sum isn't feasible, propose a structured payment plan. Determine a monthly payment amount that fits your budget and present it as a viable option for clearing the debt over a defined period. Emphasize your commitment to fulfilling the payment plan.

c. Seek Reduction in Total Amount Owed: If your financial situation is dire, consider negotiating a reduction in the total amount owed. Explain your financial hardship and present supporting documents if available. Offer to pay a reduced amount as a final settlement.

Step 4: Document and Validate Agreements

Once an agreement is reached, ensure that all negotiated terms are documented in writing. Include details such as the settlement amount, payment schedule, and any other relevant terms. Request a written confirmation from the debt collector or creditor to solidify the agreement.

Step 5: Fulfill Your Commitments

Honor the negotiated agreement by making payments promptly and in accordance with the agreed-upon terms. Keep track of your payments and retain copies of all correspondence and receipts. This will serve as evidence of your compliance.

Key points to remember when dealing with Debt Collectors and Creditors

- Conduct thorough research: Before entering into negotiations, gather information about your rights as a debtor, applicable laws, and regulations. Understanding your rights can empower you during negotiations and prevent any potential violations.

- Keep emotions in check: Negotiations can be stressful, but it's important to maintain a calm and composed demeanor. Emotions can hinder effective communication and compromise the outcome. Stay focused on the facts and your desired resolution.

- Request debt validation: If you have any doubts about the validity of the debt or the accuracy of the information, you can request debt validation. Debt collectors must provide evidence that you owe the debt, including details of the original creditor and the amount owed. Use a debt validation letter template to make the request in writing.

- Ask for payment plan flexibility: If the initially proposed payment plan seems unmanageable, don't hesitate to negotiate for more favorable terms. You can request a lower monthly payment, an extended repayment period, or adjusted interest rates. The goal is to find a solution that aligns with your financial capabilities.

- Be prepared to negotiate multiple times: Negotiations may involve back-and-forth discussions. Be patient and willing to engage in multiple rounds of negotiations to reach a mutually acceptable agreement. Stay persistent and advocate for your best interests while maintaining open lines of communication.

- Get agreements in writing: Whenever you reach an agreement with a debt collector or creditor, ensure that all terms are documented in writing. This includes the settlement amount, payment schedule, and any other agreed-upon terms. Written agreements provide clarity and protection for both parties involved.

- Keep records of all communication: Maintain detailed records of every interaction, including dates, times, names of representatives, and summaries of the discussions. Retain copies of letters, emails, and any supporting documents exchanged during the negotiation process. These records can be invaluable if any disputes arise in the future.

- Consider seeking professional assistance: If negotiations become complex or overwhelming, you may want to consider seeking help from credit counseling agencies or legal professionals specializing in debt negotiation. They can provide guidance, representation, and additional strategies to assist you in achieving a favorable outcome.

Negotiating with debt collectors and creditors requires open communication, persistence, and a clear understanding of your financial situation. By following the step-by-step process outlined in this chapter, you can work towards resolving your debt while potentially securing more favorable terms. Remember, it's crucial to remain proactive, honest, and respectful throughout the negotiation process.

Note: It's recommended to consult with legal professionals or credit counseling agencies for personalized advice and guidance tailored to your specific situation.

Step 9: Dealing with a Subpoena and Facing Legal Action

Receiving a subpoena and being faced with a debt collector or creditor taking you to court can be a stressful experience. While I cannot provide legal advice, I can guide you through the general process. It's important to consult with an attorney to fully understand your rights and obligations. In this chapter, we will provide an overview of the steps you may need to take if you find yourself in this situation.

Section 1: Understanding the Subpoena

1. Read the subpoena carefully:

When you receive a subpoena, carefully read through the document to understand its purpose and what is being requested of you. Take note of the date and location of the court hearing or deposition.

2. Retain legal representation:

Consider seeking the assistance of an attorney experienced in debt collection or civil litigation. They can provide guidance, protect your rights, and help you navigate the legal process.

Section 2: Gathering and Organizing Documentation

1. Gather all relevant documents:

Collect any documents related to the debt, including loan agreements, payment records, correspondence, and any other evidence that may support your case. It's essential to have a clear understanding of the facts surrounding the debt.

2. Organize your documents:

Ensure that your documents are organized and easily accessible. Label and categorize them in a logical order to facilitate their presentation during court proceedings.

Section 3: Preparing Your Defense

1. Consult with your attorney:

Work closely with your attorney to develop a solid defense strategy. They will help you understand the legal options available and guide you through the necessary steps.

2. Review the plaintiff's claims:

Carefully review the claims made by the debt collector or creditor. Identify any inconsistencies or errors that could weaken their case.

3. Prepare counterarguments:

Based on the evidence you've gathered and in consultation with your attorney, develop counterarguments to challenge the claims made against you. Identify any legal defenses that may apply to your situation.

Section 4: Court Proceedings

1. Attend court hearings:

Appear at all court hearings as required by the subpoena. Failing to attend could result in unfavorable judgments against you.

2. Present your case:

Present your defense in a clear and organized manner. Follow the guidance of your attorney regarding the best approach to address the plaintiff's claims and present your evidence.

3. Follow court rules and procedures:

Adhere to all court rules and procedures, such as submitting documents on time, following courtroom etiquette, and addressing the judge and opposing counsel respectfully.

Section 5: Settlement and Negotiation

1. Explore settlement options:

Consider exploring settlement negotiations with the debt collector or creditor. Your attorney can help facilitate these discussions and potentially reach a mutually beneficial agreement.

2. Evaluate potential outcomes:

Work closely with your attorney to evaluate the potential outcomes of the case, considering the evidence, legal arguments, and other factors. This will help you make informed decisions throughout the process.

Conclusion:

Dealing with a subpoena and facing legal action from a debt collector or creditor can be complex and challenging. It is crucial to consult with an attorney who can provide personalized guidance based on your specific circumstances. By carefully reviewing the subpoena, organizing your documents, preparing a strong defense, and following court procedures, you can navigate the legal process more effectively. Remember, this chapter is a general overview, and seeking professional legal advice is essential to protect your rights and ensure the best possible outcome in your case.

I. 100 Tips to Building Credit

1. Pay your bills on time to avoid late payment penalties and negative marks on your credit report.

2. Set up automatic payments or reminders to ensure timely payments.

3. Keep your credit card balances low to maintain a healthy credit utilization ratio.

4. Aim to use no more than 10% of your available credit limit.

5. Regularly review your credit reports from all three major credit bureaus (Experian, Equifax, and TransUnion).

6. Dispute any errors or inaccuracies you find on your credit reports.

7. Keep old credit accounts open to maintain a longer credit history.

8. Avoid opening multiple new credit accounts within a short period.

9. Build a positive credit history by responsibly using credit.

10. Consider becoming an authorized user on someone else's credit card to benefit from their positive credit history.

11. Avoid co-signing loans or credit cards unless you are fully aware of the risks.

12. Be cautious when closing credit accounts, as it can impact your credit utilization ratio.

13. Pay off high-interest debts first to save money and improve your credit utilization.

14. Contact creditors if you're having trouble making payments to explore possible repayment plans or alternatives.

15. Be mindful of debt settlement companies that promise quick fixes but may have adverse consequences.

16. Understand the statute of limitations on debts in your state, as it can affect legal actions taken by creditors.

17. Avoid excessive credit inquiries, as they can negatively impact your credit score.

18. Regularly check your credit card and bank statements for any unauthorized charges.

19. Maintain a diverse credit mix, including credit cards, loans, and mortgages.

20. Prioritize paying off collections and charge-offs, as they have a significant impact on your credit score.

21. Negotiate with creditors to settle outstanding debts for less than the full amount owed.

22. Educate yourself about your rights under the Fair Credit Reporting Act (FCRA).

23. Understand the impact of bankruptcy on your credit and explore alternatives before considering it.

24. Be cautious when transferring balances between credit cards, as it may incur additional fees and affect your credit utilization ratio.

25. Avoid payday loans and high-interest loans, as they can lead to a cycle of debt.

26. Consider using a secured credit card to build or rebuild credit.

27. Keep your credit card balances well below the credit limit to show responsible credit management.

28. Regularly update your personal information with creditors to ensure accurate reporting.

29. Be wary of credit repair companies that make unrealistic promises or charge exorbitant fees.

30. Utilize credit monitoring services to stay informed about changes to your credit profile.

31. Use reputable websites to access your free annual credit reports.

32. Save money for emergencies to avoid relying on credit cards for unexpected expenses.

33. Avoid maxing out your credit cards, as it indicates financial strain and negatively impacts your credit score.

34. Be patient with the credit repair process, as it takes time to see significant improvements.

35. Maintain a steady income and demonstrate stability to creditors.

36. Be cautious of scams targeting individuals with poor credit looking for quick fixes.

37. Consider debt consolidation as an option to streamline multiple debts into one manageable payment.

38. Understand the factors that contribute to your credit score, such as payment history, credit utilization, length of credit history, new credit, and credit mix.

39. Avoid excessive spending and live within your means to prevent further debt accumulation.

40. Explore credit counseling services that offer guidance and support for managing debt.

41. Keep your contact information up to date to ensure timely communication with creditors.

42. Pay attention to your credit utilization ratio on individual credit cards as well, not just overall utilization.

43. Prioritize making consistent, on-time payments to positively impact your credit score over time.

44. Understand the difference between hard inquiries (which can impact your credit score) and soft inquiries (which do not affect your credit score).

45. Research and compare credit card offers to find ones that align with your financial goals and credit-building needs.

46. Avoid closing your oldest credit card account, as it can shorten your credit history.

47. Keep credit card accounts active by using them occasionally and making timely payments.

48. If you're struggling with debt, consider reaching out to a nonprofit credit counseling agency for assistance.

49. Avoid using credit cards for cash advances, as they often come with high fees and interest rates.

50. Use online tools and resources to track your credit score progress over time.

51. Keep a record of all communication with creditors, including dates, names, and details discussed.

52. Educate yourself about the rights and protections provided by the Consumer Financial Protection Bureau (CFPB).

53. Avoid applying for multiple credit cards within a short period, as it can raise red flags to lenders.

54. Seek professional advice from a reputable credit counselor or financial advisor if needed.

55. Be cautious when transferring balances to a new credit card with an introductory 0% APR offer, as it may come with balance transfer fees.

56. Consider freezing your credit to prevent unauthorized access or identity theft.

57. Understand the impact of student loans on your credit and explore options for repayment or deferment.

58. Review your credit card statements for any recurring subscriptions you no longer use and cancel them to save money.

59. Keep your credit card information secure and avoid sharing it with unauthorized parties.

60. Understand the concept of credit aging and how it can positively affect your credit score over time.

61. Make sure your credit card balances are reported accurately to the credit bureaus.

62. Avoid making large purchases or taking on new credit obligations before applying for a major loan, such as a mortgage or auto loan.

63. Monitor your credit utilization ratio on each individual credit card to ensure none are excessively high.

64. Consider credit counseling programs that can help you create a budget and manage your debts effectively.

65. Be cautious of companies that offer to create a new credit identity for you, as this is illegal and can lead to severe consequences.

66. Utilize apps and tools that provide credit score monitoring and alerts for any changes or suspicious activity.

67. Read and understand the terms and conditions of any credit card or loan agreement before signing or accepting.

68. Be proactive in addressing any financial hardships with creditors rather than ignoring the issue.

69. Understand the impact of foreclosure on your credit and explore options to prevent it.

70. Seek legal advice if you believe you have been a victim of identity theft or fraudulent activity affecting your credit.

71. Pay attention to the impact of authorized user accounts on your credit report, as they can affect your credit score positively or negatively.

72. Review your credit report for any outdated or incorrect personal information and request updates as necessary.

73. Understand the difference between a hard inquiry (initiated by a creditor) and a soft inquiry (initiated by you or a third party).

74. Consider seeking financial education resources to enhance your knowledge and skills in managing credit.

75. Be cautious of payday lenders and their high-interest rates, as they can lead to a cycle of debt.

76. Keep your credit card balances well below the credit limit to demonstrate responsible credit utilization.

77. Avoid taking on unnecessary debt, even if you have the available credit.

78. Understand the implications of debt consolidation loans, as they may come with fees and affect your credit.

79. Research and compare interest rates, fees, and rewards programs before applying for new credit cards.

80. Avoid closing multiple credit accounts within a short period, as it may negatively impact your credit score.

81. Pay attention to the credit limits on your credit cards and consider requesting increases if necessary.

82. Keep track of your credit card due dates and set reminders to avoid late payments.

83. Be cautious of credit repair scams that promise instant credit score improvements.

84. Avoid using your credit cards for impulse purchases and unnecessary expenses.

85. Seek guidance from a housing counselor if you're struggling with mortgage payments or facing foreclosure.

86. Consider paying off small debts first to gain a sense of accomplishment and build momentum.

87. Monitor your credit card statements for any unauthorized charges or fraudulent activity.

88. Understand the implications of debt settlement on your credit score and overall financial situation.

89. Review your credit reports for any accounts that you don't recognize or that may be the result of identity theft.

90. Keep copies of all correspondence with creditors and credit reporting agencies for your records.

91. Pay attention to your credit score fluctuations and seek to understand the factors behind them.

92. Consider applying for a secured credit card if you're unable to qualify for a traditional unsecured card.

93. Be cautious of using your credit cards to finance a lifestyle beyond your means.

94. Take advantage of credit score simulators to understand how certain actions may affect your credit score.

95. Avoid applying for multiple credit cards or loans simultaneously, as it can negatively impact your credit.

96. Understand the impact of debt-to-income ratio on your creditworthiness and financial stability.

97. Regularly review your credit card terms and conditions for any changes or updates.

98. Keep your credit card balances manageable by paying more than the minimum payment whenever possible.

99. Stay informed about changes in credit laws and regulations that may affect your rights and protections.

100. Remember that improving your credit takes time, patience, and consistent effort. Stay committed to your goals and continue practicing responsible credit habits.

II. Understanding Credit Score Calculation

Your credit score plays a crucial role in determining your financial health and ability to secure loans or credit. Understanding how credit scores are calculated can help you make informed decisions and take actions to improve your score.

Section 1: Key Credit Score Factors

1. Payment History:

Your payment history has the most significant impact on your credit score. It reflects whether you've paid your bills on time, including credit card payments, loans, and other debts. Late payments, delinquencies, and defaults can negatively affect your score.

2. Credit Utilization:

Credit utilization refers to the amount of credit you're using compared to your total credit limit. It's important to keep your credit utilization ratio low, ideally below 10%. High utilization suggests financial strain and may lower your credit score.

3. Length of Credit History:

The length of your credit history plays a role in determining your creditworthiness. A longer credit history demonstrates a track record of responsible credit management. If you're just starting, it may take time to build a positive credit history.

4. Credit Mix:

Creditors consider the types of credit you have, such as credit cards, loans, mortgages, and retail accounts. A diverse mix of credit can positively impact your score, showing your ability to manage different types of credit responsibly.

5. New Credit:

Opening multiple new credit accounts within a short period can raise concerns for lenders. Each new account results in a hard inquiry on your credit report, which may temporarily lower your score. Be mindful of applying for new credit unless necessary.

Section 2: Credit Score Calculation Models

1. FICO Score:

The FICO score is a widely used credit scoring model. It considers the factors mentioned above, assigning specific weights to each. Payment history carries the most significant weight, followed by credit utilization, length of credit history, credit mix, and new credit.

2. VantageScore:

VantageScore is another popular credit scoring model that also evaluates creditworthiness. It considers similar factors as the FICO score but may weigh them differently. VantageScore 4.0, for example, places a greater emphasis on consistent payment history.

Section 3: Credit Score Improvement Strategies

1. Pay bills on time:

Consistently making timely payments is crucial for maintaining a good credit score. Set reminders, automate payments, or create a budget to ensure you never miss a payment.

2. Reduce credit utilization:

Lowering your credit utilization ratio can have a positive impact on your score. Paying down debts and keeping credit card balances low can help achieve this goal.

CRACKING THE CODE: TO CREDIT REPAIR

3. Monitor your credit report:

Regularly review your credit report for inaccuracies or fraudulent activity. Dispute any errors you find to prevent them from negatively affecting your credit score.

4. Build a positive credit history:

Establishing a solid credit history takes time, but starting small can help. Open a credit card or loan account, make small purchases, and pay them off in full and on time.

5. Be mindful of new credit applications:

Avoid unnecessary credit applications, as each inquiry can temporarily lower your credit score. Apply for credit only when necessary and when you're confident of approval.

Understanding how credit scores are calculated empowers you to take control of your financial well-being. By focusing on improving key credit factors, staying vigilant about your credit report, and adopting responsible credit management habits, you can work towards building and maintaining a healthy credit score. Remember, it's a gradual process, but your efforts will pay off in the long run.

Note: Credit scoring models may vary, and it's important to stay informed about the specific scoring system used in your country or region.

Conclusion

Congratulations on completing "Cracking the Code: Credit Repair and the Path to Financial Independence" You have taken a significant step toward reclaiming control of your financial future. This book has provided you with the knowledge and tools to clean up your credit without the need for expensive attorneys or credit repair companies.

Throughout this journey, you have learned the incredibly easy process that professionals use to remove derogatory items from credit reports. From charge-offs to bankruptcies, late payments to collection accounts, you now possess the knowledge to tackle them all. By following the step-by-step instructions, you have empowered yourself to improve your credit from poor to excellent, with FICO scores soaring above 700.

The power of dispute letters has become evident, as they allow you to challenge inaccurate information and hold creditors accountable. The four dispute letter templates provided have given you a powerful arsenal to assert your rights and demand accurate credit reporting. You have equipped yourself to confidently respond to credit reporting agencies' correspondence and ensure that your voice is heard.

Remember, this book has revealed things that creditors don't want you to know. You now possess the knowledge to save money and bring yourself financial freedom. No longer must you dream of a better life; you can make it a reality.

As you embark on your credit repair journey, keep in mind the importance of perseverance and discipline. It may take time to see the full results of your efforts, but every step you take brings you closer to your goal. Stay proactive, stay organized, and stay committed.

Lastly, always remember that improving your credit is not just about numbers on a report. It is about regaining control of your financial well-being, opening doors to better opportunities, and achieving the life you desire. Take what you have learned from this book and apply it consistently in your financial journey.

May this book serve as a guide, a source of inspiration, and a catalyst for your financial success. Wishing you a future filled with financial freedom and prosperity!

One Last Thing

Thank you once again for taking the time to read my book. If you have found it enjoyable or beneficial, I would greatly appreciate it if you could spare a few moments to write a brief review on Amazon Kindle. Your support means a lot to me, and it truly makes a difference. I genuinely value your feedback as it enables me to grow and enhance my work in the future. Thank you once more for your time and consideration.

www.ingramcontent.com/pod-product-compliance
Lightning Source LLC
Chambersburg PA
CBHW070848220526
45466CB00005B/1928